Everywhere and Nowhere

Annie Farley

BookLeaf Publishing

India | USA | UK

Presentation by *BookLeaf Publishing*

Web: www.bookleafpub.com

E-mail: info@bookleafpub.com

ISBN: 9789363317529

First edition 2024

This is dedicated to my friends, my tribe. You have been there for me in the darkest moments and have celebrated every single win with me. I love you.

PREFACE

This collection is for anyone who feels lost in their own life. It is the joy and pain of rediscovering who you are and always have been. It is the highest highs and courageous moments, to the lowest lows of loss and self doubt. It is all about this human experience we are all sharing.

Reborn

I feel a rebirth
a shedding of skin
Release of the old for
New to begin
roots burst from my feet
anchor me deep
The empty womb
That just won't keep
butterflies in my stomach
have taken to rest
flowers have bloomed
Amid my chest
My mouth knows the words
To call in the rain
And my eyes will never
Be closed again
Limbs spring from my crown
Reaching toward glory
A tired body has
Rewritten it's story

I Am the Problem

Oh the freedom
I've just enough slack
I run and I run
something's holding me back
Giving all that I have
I pull and i strain
Pleading with God
only to be pulled again
This is the time
I know that I'm done
I scratch and claw
I run and I run
I dig in, lean in
hold ground gained
pull at the tether
That's keeping me chained
I'm more than this!
I scream through my teeth
Look at me! Look at me!
See what's beneath
Just let me go
Aren't you tired too?
Through weary exhaustion I hear
It was never me, always you

Is Knowledge Power?

If knowledge is power
why do I feel weak
There's safety in numbers
But it's truth I seek
I move further away
The more that I know
Floating above
With you below
This knowing binds my heart
Alone, I don't want to go
But it is comfortable
It's what I know
If knowledge is power
why do I feel weak
I have unlocked the stories
That have kept me meek
No longer scared and small
I embrace my birthright
The truth of my grace
Out of the dark. Into the light

The Choice

If you could do it all again
Would you?
Would you hold your heart captive, never
exposed
Or share your heart wildly and suffer the blows
Would you?
This chance is yours
Would you live life small, afraid of the stars
Or live life bravely and relish the scars
Would you?
This dance is yours
Would you help others along the way
Or ignore, abandon and push them away
Would you?
This choice is yours
Would you speak of joy, of love, of truth
Or wait for someone to show you the proof
Would you?
This voice is yours
If you could do it all again
Would you?

I Surrender

Surrendering does not mean
 to the void, the darkness
The nothing, the non existence
Surrendering does mean
To the everything, the love
The pain, the connection
The full existence
Every breeze across your skin feels like
whispers of friends
Every moment of deep laughter
Shatters the separation of time
Every tear drops with the weight
Of a thousand heartbreaks
Every "I love you" heals the hearts
Of generations without end
Surrender, let's begin

Comfortably Taking Up Space

We are learning to hold space
To lean in, go further
Slow down, maybe stop
Take things at our own pace
The world says move faster,
it doesn't matter
You against them, one winner
Only embrace what pays
But value is defined
By the things we cherish
Things cultivated and loved
Gifts of the body, heart and mind
We will not race this rat
We will not give away our power
We will not compare or shrink
We deserve so much more that
We will sit in our grace
We will expand and expand
Until my edges dissolve yours
Comfortably taking up space

After The Storm

A time of quiet between the storms
A moment to collect your scattered dreams
A stillness to embrace what remains
An anticipation, a tension of storms to come
A buzzing, tingling of potential
The first drops bathe your skin
Open your arms and dance in the rain
welcome the turbulent change
Ask for a cleansing to begin
Let the deluge in, flooding your cells,
filling your lungs
know that this weather too shall pass
And you will emerge anew
To begin again

A Life to Unfold

Time to unpack
This case is filled to bursting
Pushing the edges, straining the locks
Do I really need all this stuff
Or can I be done carrying rocks?
Those pants I save
For when I am smaller
Whisper there is too much of me to love
That dress that I bought
Because it looked so good on her
Still has the tags, too scared to try on
Reminds me that I don't belong
The baggy sweats that hide who I am
Hold me in comfort and invisibility
Safest to hide, false security
But oh the t-shirt, soft and worn
Feels like a second skin
Light on my body and smells like him
Reaffirms I am wanted, cherished even
So maybe a few things can stay
But I'll lighten the load
Keep all the sweet things
Of a life left to unfold.

Breath New Life

Breathe in, breathe out
The mind learns to quiet
It's leading the way
Breathe in, breathe out
Through blackened hallways
Closed door upon closed door
The breath blows them all open
Breathe in, breathe out
Spaces too long kept in the dark
Receive light and fresh air
Understanding, comfort and care
Breathe in, breathe out
With tenderness,
You hold yourself there
A million pieces coming together at once
Breathe in, breathe out
I'm here for you it soothes
Take my hand and walk with me
You are me and I am you
Breathe in, breathe out
A rush of love and certainty
Washes the halls
Clearing the way, you're worthy
Breathe in, breathe out
Open your eyes, the world feels new

You're in the same place,
but not the same you
Breathe in, breathe out

Transmutation

The anger is acid, on the edges it glows
Larger and larger it infinitely grows
Claiming, consuming all in it's path
This layer of protection, an unseen aftermath
A flash of pain, felt from below
Drops me in sadness, an endless black hole
Into the darkness, I fall and I fall
Walls closing in, for once feeling it all
With a heaving heart, acceptance partaking
Understanding this hurt is of my own making
healing waters flow, a glimmer of light
I float to the surface, escaping the night
No longer weighed down or playing the game
I know this feeling, I cry out it's name
Like a seed breaking bonds, becoming a flower
The feeling transmuted, pain into power.

Lifeline

Walking the knife edge of panic
hounds of fear on my heels
Darkness oppressive, closing in
Fingers clutching, clawing my ribs
The liquid air, filling my chest
Limbs frozen, an eternal hug
Hollow echoes, silenced cries
I fall and I fall, scrabbling for purchase
Desperation oozes from within
A lifeline, a hand thrust in the dark
A beam of light, shows me the way
I kind word, an embrace of understanding
aloneness retreats, taking pain's hand
Four words are oxygen to my gasping heart
Repeated again and again
I'm here for you

Pinocchio's Realization

13

When did Pinocchio realize he wasn't real?
When did he understand
Wood and string and cloth can't feel?
He could dance and he could sing
When was the moment, the flash
There is something more to being
Did he fear what reality brings
That all of his wants, his wishes and dreams
Could hurt him, break him, cut him like string
safety does not lay in someone else's hands
Saying their lines and dancing their dance this
unknown life, these unmapped lands
Are scary, intense and unruly
To really live is to take the risk,
Learn to love, feel the pain, honor yourself truly.

Goodbye

Sometimes when people leave they don't make a
sound, no footsteps on the floor,
no restrained tears, just empty space where you
were pretty sure they were before

The Hands of the Sculptor

I feel my power rise like the morning sun
full of intensity, life giving, soul serving passion.
It fills the space between limiting fear and
limitless courage, lifting eyes upward, thoughts
overflowing the page. Will you ever know the
peace of your wisdom, the touch of your grace?
It calms rough waters, it quiets the space
between death and rebirth, the in between
alchemy. My being has shifted, down to my
cells, no longer recognizable, I'm someone else.
Your sculptors hands have moulded, encouraged,
shown beauty in seeing. No longer conforming,
contorting, just whole hearted being. There is no
goodbye in this world any longer, you are part of
my structure, my foundation made stronger. I
carry you in my breath, my bones and my blood,
whispering poetry, songs in my heart, always
there, my love

If I Could Take This From You, I Would

As you cried I held your tears in my hands, how can something so small carry so much weight? As the words cut their way out of you I felt myself bleed, I would take this from you if I could, I would swallow it whole, devour the beast that casts long shadows so the sun could shine from your eyes again

Acceptance

When you stop fighting
the storms raging inside
and let them pass,
you can appreciate
the powerful clearing left behind,
revel in the brightness and warmth
of the returning sun.
When you embrace your thoughts
and color your words with love
you welcome the rhythm within
 and our soul dances freely

Burn

I'm not waiting for anyone to build
me up in the perfect stack,
I'm the goddamn match
it just took a minute to catch
up to my potential my glorious now
not a minute wasted
breathe up all the air in the room and burn,
fucking buuuuuuuuurn
no longer hiding my flame
but lighting the world,
igniting others along the way
let's burn so beautiful
that they can't look away
let's sear our image onto their hearts
so they never forget
who they are

The Cure

Say it
Whisper it to the unbelieving hearts
I want you, I need you, I love you
And all your mismatched parts
Exclaim it to all the courageous souls
Keep going, don't quit, I'm proud of you
Chase your dreams, your life, your goals
Remind the lost and unsure
You are safe, I am here, you are whole
This world needs more words not less, that is the
the cure

Adopt a Highway

I am collecting pieces
of myself along the way
Like picking up debris
along the scenic byway
Big ones, small ones,
light ones, heavy ones.
Pieces that have been missing
far too long
new and interesting pieces
Alter the existing landscape
horizons shift before me
So many possibilities
I will forever be collecting pieces
of myself along the way

Bring on the Rain

Today I danced in the rain
let it soak through my temperament
and drip away disillusionment
Oh the colors made more vibrant
when the earth falls silent
I danced in the rain
Until I was free again
Uninhibited I twirled and spun
No more emotions to outrun
I welcome them in, drench me in feeling
Soak me in love, pain, hope, faith unfaltering
Bring on the rain

I Am

I am earth and sky and everything in between I find myself in rain and wildflowers stretching toward the sun I am darkness and light power and pain I am the silence between notes the tension that sings I am a tree in the wind learning to bend but trusting my roots I am the flow of the river rushing home but tasting the dirt I am a child taking first steps I am an old man taking last breaths I am the love that expands from my heart outward finding your edges and grasping your hand I become we only to become one again I am you and you are me

9 789363 317529